WHAT IS THE REAL STORY?

poems by

BARBARA FLUG COLIN

Finishing Line Press
Georgetown, Kentucky

WHAT IS THE REAL STORY?

Copyright © 2025 by Barbara Flug Colin
ISBN 979-8-89990-063-1 First Edition
All rights reserved under International and Pan-American Copyright Conventions. No part of this book may be reproduced in any manner whatsoever without written permission from the publisher, except in the case of brief quotations embodied in critical articles and reviews.

Special thanks to Arthur Vogelsang

Publisher: Leah Huete de Maines
Editor: Christen Kincaid
Cover Art: Eric Drooker
Author Photo: Raymond Saperstein
Cover Design: Grace Hopkins: www.gracehopkins.squarespace.com

Order online: www.finishinglinepress.com
also available on amazon.com

Author inquiries and mail orders:
Finishing Line Press
PO Box 1626
Georgetown, Kentucky 40324
USA

Contents

The sound 1

Whose is the real story? 3

I can't get the plot 6

Return…Go back…*One must go back* 7

Did you find out? 16

What is the Real Story? 19

stories characters plot 23

the sound 28

The sound 31

What is the real story? 34

The sound 43

I had to find signs 44

The sound 46

*Bold italicized fragments of Henri Matisse quotes are from *Matisse on Art, Revised Edition: Edited by Jack Flam* (University of California Press, 1995), as are non-quoted bold fragments, which are loosely based on Matisse's statements.

*For our family,
past, present and future*

The sound

disturbs you when you notice how it ruins the silence.
Distant, formless or not heard at all then.

But to the child the sound is air. The adult returning hears
a dark weight in sea air outside your home, language beginning

an edifice to be inside one room, then many. Maybe you left home
to be closer to the sound outside. Loud now. Tracked electric

moving form to see. Not to be sea, endless, uncontrolled.
The sound is to understand what you withstand. Or why the shadows

or what they mean. Maybe language is to feel its conjugation.
So nothing here will return us to before…

...1903...

Great grandfather's home
burned down so his family leaves
for our other great grandfather's home,

a close Polish town where dad is born,
but the home is ravaged by thieves
so they move back into

the rebuilt bigger first…

Whose is the real story?

Dad's five sisters and one brother told us versions,
but he never told us any of this before he died, at 57,
so what did dad feel leaving his Eden, ***1905-6**

Joy of Life or when Russian soldiers filled him, four,
with liquor, or at five, crossing Poland, Belgium,
sea to Ellis Island without a passport?

Our story is family is the mansion that remains.
Henri Matisse's is: *I remained the same…from Joy of Life…
to this…*My story is, our father feels he is this mansion

he is walking past, in Brooklyn,
not thinking this is May 19, **1940**…my …*Dream*
on this wide tree-lined Manhattan Beach street

contains much…open to sun…*like alas many of my paintings*…

Feeling...

Two sons...The nine-year-old palm softness in his.
The baby in the carriage he pushes.
His adored wife, home, deeper in Brooklyn, with me, unborn.

He was a self-confident, too curious Jewish child in Poland...
his oldest sister said. He is a self-confident man, squat, muscular, handsome, thirty-five... not thinking about fire burning down the Isbica home, thieves in the Zamosc, next.

But they arrived in America.

Home became a Brooklyn climb up from Powell Street to Hinsdale to Sheepshead Bay he just crossed.
The wooden footbridge...

its sign...

DO NOT MAKE FAST
TO THIS BRIDGE

his big strides defied

to get to the height. Rich, Jewish. He earned, by day. Night college, law, accounting schools. She, a master teacher, earned too. They, eloping nudists...*The Pink Nude...knowing myself a colourist* socialists hitchhiking the U.S.A. Then Paris. She, pregnant. They returned home.

FOR SALE. He enters...

Here was once a sensational garden...*the small flower that never turns out as expected...* centered between bay and sea, then a bootlegger built this brick mansion to impress his actress mistress, then the garden divided, concrete sidewalks squared, roads tarred for homes.

This home, the original…***white, pure…empty.***

Biggest on the block. Now abandoned. Ramshackle. Ruined.
Four stories. Rooms beyond rooms. Hand-tooled oak banisters.
Green Wedgewood ceiling beams. Ballroom. Our mother will cry.
Yell. Scream at him. But he buys

this mansion he is inside.

I can't get the plot!

I tell mom, like a child, at 48, January 1988,
Joan Sutherland's final Met performance, *Lucia*.

In Shun Lee, mom, 81, widowed at 55, swills her nightly
5 p.m. Harvey's Bristol Cream from her silver flask,
sends back her egg roll, too cold. Tells me her story.

Lucia di Lammermoor was her first record, at nine.
Her bankrupt mother, widowed before she was born,
gave her six children education, opera, religion.

She tells me two versions of *Lucia*. I tell her one version
of yesterday...my psychoanalyst persists...I must find out........
my beginning....trauma....... ....His room is dim...

...and a smell...stale cigar smoke...leather chaise...curvy arms, legs...
tan Ralph Lauren Victorian...an upright chair I choose opposite
him... seated tall but slightly leaning toward me as if relaxed behind
his desk...

...black...oak...white-flecked navy tie. Navy jacket. Face...
sometimes handsome, framed as it is by slicked back white hair,
azure eyes...The rest: nose, mouth, ears...I never notice...because

they don't move...he doesn't speak...
much...except...for his
recurring theme:

...Return...Go back......*One must go back...*

Parents' Brooklyn bedroom in winter, 1940's

The room is dim.
Our parents' bedroom is dim
because memory has not yet turned up the lights.

Or memory pulled the cord from the china chandelier.
Or memory will always remain dim.
The memory of the view from their bed is clear.

A smaller windowed outer room,
windowed from this room,
has pines looking in, blocking sun.

I dream... *meditation...on...*voyeur pine
dropped the lost gleaming needle *the expression*
of a dream... I must find.

Parents' Connecticut bedroom in summer, 1940's

Upstairs, their rear bedroom.
Three windowed walls open to green,
open to... *reality*...day and night summer air,

open to sun, rain...they don't care.
Or that a continuous *sss* of wasps
vibrates their screens.

February 1988 Carnegie Hall

Orchestra members walk off stage playing Haydn's *Farewell*.
I walk mom to her 59th street apartment.

How to find the truth,...***an essential truth...***
I say... ***disengaged from...appearance of objects..***
...beginning...trauma...proof?

Everybody has traumas, mom says,
looking down on Central
Park skaters circling.

Brooklyn home in winter, 1940's

In memory, bodies of water are...***each work of art...***my body. In retrospect Sheepshead Bay had no boats, was not right-angled for cars to enter our peninsula, Manhattan Beach, blocked out in...***a collection of sign's...***alphabet...***invented...***streets, Amherst, Beaumont, Coleridge, Dover.

Exeter, ours. Our corner home midway between bay and sea.

Connecticut home in summer, 1940's

Our home, on Easton Road in Westport, Connecticut, is in Stonybrook,
our summer community, once socialist, no property lines…***freedom***
You need more land, take some of mine….***of invention…***

Daddy bought acres in '34 for practically nothing.
Our ancient blue-trimmed white wooden farmhouse
Aaron Burr hid in. Walk into anyone's home.

Drive through our colony. The one tarred road,
a U, begins and ends with a brook,
each with a wooden bridge.

Cross as you smell what you hear in moist air. Aspiration.
We swim nude in our private brook,
dammed falling

from Eden, fed by the big brook, upstream, beside four clay
tennis courts for all members, all live inside the colony.
We don't. We're the only members across Easton Road.

In dreams
mind is home
across from body.

Away from home
I know I left a burner on,
I rush to save time,
be first in line,
but I can't return
to the first fire in time.....*a distant fire*......

May, 1988, younger brother Bud drives me to Manhattan Beach,
our Jewish neighborhood anti-Semite railroad magnate Austin
Corbin built, restricted, diverted his trains to the next neighborhood,
Brighton Beach.

At Corbin Place, the threshold………..to memory's curved beach steps
*...never...a curve……without...its relationship to...*too wide, white,
*the vertical...*hot to descend…to sea…

Where public sand ends, we enter our private Brighton Beach Baths:
arched bandstand, rectangular tennis court and elevated pool

return the child feeling contained,
fenced in, elevated
looking back,

down and out to sea.
And turning the opposite way
I see the reality of my dream.

The white eye coming through darkness to attack
was headlights on the el trains coming at me
from New York City.

My dream of the train overcoming me
on track
is the reality that it never makes contact.

The trains fenced from me come close,
then black snakes left around the final bend
to Coney Island.

We walk to the end of the block, Lincoln Savings Bank.
Our vault was in its basement, I say, then we cross west to...

Memory………..darkness...brake-sparked…below...el tracks...
…………bass……..guttural trills………….tar……melt smell...

Ground is moving shadows of trains you can't see, enter, be, expressing nameless sound heard in childhood.

Before the el, facing it, left, deepest in: sea. Before blocks. Below the el, looking up to it: infinity, between tracks.

June 1988, Mom in the MoMA. Blue silk Gucci,
white teased hair: How's the psychoanalyst?

Behind her red blares from Matisse's *Harmony in Red* dining room.
The servant leaning over a fruit bowl on the red table has puffy hair
like mom and like white trees outside a glass-paned background of
green bush, grass, yellow and violet flower dots, pink house, blue sky...

Me: I got rid of him…Can analyze myself like Matisse
says to………**illuminate the fog that surrounds us…**His

table wall the same red material
veined by blue arabesques to protect
blue baskets of blue flowers whose
eyes look out at us needing to see this

inside out Matisse is
this masked uniformed servant
composing his feast inside
opening to pure white

blossoming arabesque trees
or wild flowering yellows and violets freed
from curvy background green
cliff in blue eternity

and right-angled black-roofed pink-
skinned edifice cut off
left at canvas
edge…

Did you find out?

mom asks.

He's finding out. His past emerging in forms changing
since his first dim dining room, to his second, self-reflecting
from sun through a window, on crystal. Then this windowed
background...

Me: No...but I will.

...like a painting hung, left, in the upper 1/6th of this painting of a red room. Like a body left in his mind. Left out, far back, black-roofed pink house below blue mean sky. Closer are curvy white blossoming trees, grass...

outside, like an opponent across a net. But in and out a perfect match. Curves/right-angles, reds/greens, yellows/violets...blues...oppose/complement each other. Matisse's forms of himself. Shaped spectrum of his nature. In harmony.

Mom: How?

Me: Snapshots are stuck in my mind.

Of some body I am within first dim room or inside
neighborhood two Brighton Beach arches, rectangles or
in neighborhood three Coney Island vehicles of circling intensity or

in Matisse's black-roofed pink rectangle prelude to being outside in whole 1909 circle *Dance* of five savage nude up close well of unformed decibels vibrating the height original darkness is

somebody I am with in
a duet dive into the night
highway. Hit

flat but intact.
Others have done the same.
There is only this road

for parallels metaphors
ladders in space
steps toward a core

to feel flight
fall in a sign:
night dive as white dove.

Mom: That's scary!

that weight on your palm,
that bird to cage
in the inn vestibule

Then rules. For innings. Points to win
hit and run repeats of first seed
in time to return home, base,

so this left-right returning across
this endless diving board below
movie projector sun *I*

will make myself my own pool,
Matisse says, returning
home to recreate

pool-side sun-glassed voyeur watching
from her yellow beach chair as background
yellow wildflowers call from contoured hills:

you can't dive in. **on white paper horizontal**
on burlap walls, figures in and out...
myself, my own pool.

What is the Real Story?

Look! Sport is art…as brother narrates his
story of Ellsworth Kelly's *Palm* and *Tennis Court*
as human body reflection, whose

1949 primitive body reliefs strung
like a tennis racket, his 1957 *Palm*,
the human palm beginning

tennis, the medieval monk repelling the animal
fur ball, the original football, pig bladder or
human head soccer ball…

It takes time to construct body like a cathedral…
Matisse said…
being driven to be

the vehicle driven to recreate past time
to control its arch reflection
in a portable language

any body
to be
out in it.

Bud: At 42 I'm going to law school.
Me: Why?

Bud: I was walking down a street
going nowhere,

needed no one,
wanted nothing.

I dream I see what nothing is.

And what nothing is to be.
Infinity designed. A sign. Prostrate.
Set upright. An hourglass. A figure eight.

I dream I am the beginning darkness coming to light
the wild beast I am circling the ring I am
pulling the reins too tight. I grow a third eye.

The three eyes are O's
of ice melting to nothing in solution.
The three I's began when black swan got in

to form circle pond to open forest to sun,
wooden arms, legs attaching, blush being painted on.
Strings pulling marionette upright.

I see with my third eye some
body I am longing for, left deepest in,
coming to me, stopped midway across the desert.

My center out in the center, sun too hot,
letters rain for her to feel the fall
of solution in form, dimensions she bends to touch.

She does not understand what she stands under,
withstands or why she must enter her first red engineless train
before she can come to me.

To feel being inside herself.
To see what is
out its glass pane.

I dream I feel whole out in space before
grammar or laws or metaphors for
ladder steps from my core
or closest relatives
to step up or
down

from the height
of Red Mountain…

five siblings
five east west states

reunite
at Dick's home.

Day one,
he's grilling Bud,

Dick: How's law school?
Bud: Over for the summer.

Dick: Your job? Bud: Boring.
Dick: Your friends? Bud: Depressed.

Dick lectures on depression. Then,

stories characters plot…

Dick: Mom was perfect. A master teacher. (He always criticized her, alive.)
Alfie: Dad too. Perfect. (He complained dad was silent driving him to Yale.)

Me: Dad…selfless…deep… sensuous embrace…bass singing Yiddish lullabies, *Summertime*, opera. Mixing jokes, poems, business. Reciting his own poems or

Heine, Poe, Kipling: *Boots-boots-boots-boots-movin'………in…war.*
Bud: He was never in a war, they never fought, we joked, tricked, laughed, loved, happy.

Nancy: They exposed us to everything, but it all fell into boxes.
We just saw what we were supposed to, we couldn't get in or behind words.

What does sweet taste like?

I dream box inside box inside box.
I open the lid on the biggest box.
They attack.

Aspen sibling reunion day two green-hued metallic black
dining table, shellacked oval like a scarab beetle's back,
oval, like Dick's pool, outside, behind his back. Agreed,

Dick says, at the head, with contracts, we'll sell our Westport home.
Nancy beside me, we, two beetle members whose opposites,
Alfie and Bud, block the canvas on the wall behind them,

id entities, composed to reli(e)ve the emergency,
the huge Elizabeth Murray red canvas' inner pink doodles emerging
in 3-D or submerging, depending on where we are in the
conversation...

Remember your iceboat that Brooklyn winter, Alfie says, laughs.

Little Black Sambo's wild beasts circling.
Pebbles dropped by Hansel and Gretel to lead them back.

Dick, at 11, built an iceboat for Alfie, three, me, two seated on its
plank Dick shoved down our iced alley as white sheet unfurled
from broomstick mast, out our curly wrought iron gate, out, beyond
concrete sidewalk into white-eyed attack of black curvy Cadillac.

William Carlos Williams' howling fire engine.
Charles Demuth's swelling fire engine.

At five, safe inside our gate, inside my own red fire engine, I learn to
steer the circle for four outside wheels, control my naked pink rubber
ball inside my palm, jump the arc I make with my rope, arc in air as
knees pump my swing.

The figure 5 head right-angled
to keep in mind curvy body below.

Your iceboat was stuck in our alley, never budged, Alfie says. Laughs.
He has the photo.

At three, Dick says, you solicited sailors' kisses on Exeter Street.
I remember sailors walking to their base at the beach. Manhattan
Beach. Converted for war.

Coney Island circling reaching for gold rings.
Five Matisse dancers circling.

I'm three. It's Sunday. Back from Coney Island. After a shower with
daddy. Out our gate in my sailor dress. I'm a WAVE not a WAC.
Daddy's black curvy Cadillac and the el trains coming at me do not
attack.

Phallic U shapes Stonybrook, Klee's *Mask of Fear,* Kelly's *Kilometer
Marker, Playskool* mailbox slit to fit fake 3D geometric painted wood
letters. To hear the impact. As the blocks fall inside.

So I solicit sailor's kisses. At four, play with Susan in her bath,
at five, undress with Bobby in his tool shed, at six, kiss Ellwyn in
the Center Academy yard…At 12, breasts bud. Focus on tennis, dad
said…

flame burning inside living room pane, vehicles of the emergency
emerging, fire engines racing up and down the block. Gong clanging,
approaching…

…Steve in his car Dave in his basement Ted in the den…

and the tall fire chief gets in, bends down
and lifts a floorboard, smiles:

This fire is coming along well!

Rat gets up through floorboard…

Like memory, Bud said,

before the el, across Brighton Beach Avenue
from Lincoln Savings Bank, beside the Tuxedo
Movie Theater, outside Mrs. Stahl's Knishes,

we stood eating her delicious
dough-covered mush.
Smells, tastes like memory, Bud said,

facing the el

I left home in
self-reflecting els
to block sea out in relatives

mom, Evelyn, dad Samuel,
L in Lincoln Savings Bank a block away,
brook l blocked out in Brooklyn

center of self out in The Center Academy Torah El to imagine
the original being suspended nothing to be
live in

...afraid I
am the one who swallowed the sun
and black shadows are stuck in my throat

the cathedral of childhood flooded
as pigeons signaled from outside my stained glass meaning
to get in

basement emptied, the walls scathed yellow,
the floor, clean, white, still, excerpts of the birds,
feathers strewn, one bulb dangling from the ceiling…

the threshold to our neighborhood
a still well
of drowned towns

no voyeur pine outside the pane to block sun out
in the first dim room to drop pine need
el I found

in time
to remember

the sound

...below

...Brighton Beach boardwalk...slatted wood thuds above
sheltered sand cool
for bare feet to stand illicit moist salt-scented darkness light slit before

running out across endless sunned sand
diving into the height
of white falling, shattering sea...owned

...by a sign............STEEP...L...........E...CHASE...GEO...C.
T............I...L.............................YOU'S
black mustache-like hair above lascivious eyes, sadistic smile,

thick grit white teeth
as his paned edifice spewed
painted steel stallions we children rode

on outside tracks
toward sea
and back......

After *Little Black Sambo*'s story
of circling
tigers melting
to butter…

there was so much possibility to repeat the original
circling on Coney Island carousel hand-painted stallions
and reach for gold rings, symbols, like the bush outside
Matisse's **Harmony in Red** glass pane is

green as the ground it springs from to suspend
further back curvy spines for white blossoming
trees arced to protect purple and yellow flower sparks
like crumbs dropped by the child for the path back

to his red interior fury-passion veined by an origin bursting its seas
to design the canvas Matisse first named **Harmony in Blue**
but red insisted it could be in harmony with the spectrum
of his nature's savage sensational tense vibrations

civilized

as musical circle of fifths or seas seized
as O pond black swan L enters

center open to steel right-angle steps
to ascend outside this white

motel to look back across
the desert of a life to see this

       green-trained   horizon   moving   left   -right

    off

       track

for comeback-attack I dream…
the destruction of

the el
like Matisse destroys language

paints over the original 1896 child,
the blue, the penciled doodles

become cutout space in *Memory
of Oceania 1952-3* beginning in

1896: *Breton Serving Girl* serving his lost child its solution,
1905-6: Six circling *Joy of life* dancers by sea deepest in Eden,
1908: *Harmony in Red* pink right-angled house

background coming to the foreground
as oval *Dance* of five nudes,
eye sees, as mind perceives circle

to contain, in form, memory
of pure intensity, as two, closest to us,
reach toward each other, but can't attach.

The sound

remains outside your home,
a dark weight in sea air,
the real meal the servant Matisse is

waiting, patient, changing costumes, roles,
characters for her to be ***truer, more essential
to the whole.***

The sound vibrating screens it provides
for the first bright room old
sun-glassed Matisse recreates,

a pool to return solution

I left to be
inside this
holocaust train

language is
to ascend out right
in sun not

my nature before
the solution to the fall is named
the sound of falling solution before

forest center clears
primitive urges Matisse fears approaching
his canvas to ***strangle body***

white paper is
to cut slit to resist
sea flooding the cathedral

to master my body
the final solution
Matisse's wife and daughter survive

in the Resistance
Gestapo
Ravenstock

Flames burning inside…cabin I am…never to enter.
    William Carlos William's golden 5 on red fire engine.
        Fire engines racing up-down your block.

Old sick Matisse *fragile as crystal.*
    Shabbat table crystal reflects antique silver candlesticks.
        Self-reflecting Matisse dining room two crystal reflections flare

clatter or roar………I can't get the plot.
    Boys eat dark meat, chicken legs, chocolate ice cream pops. Race Lionel trains too fast.
        Girls eat white meat, chicken wings, vanilla ice cream. Watch Lionel trains crash.

In his studio songbirds caged in his childhood fly free.
    Bass-soprano-tenor-alto success stories sung by dad-mom-Dick-Alfie.
        Sensation of flight **his cutting is in his studio.**

Dick's story of what he did in sixth grade when Rothko pinned…
    Matisse pointed Lydia pinned leaf on bedroom wall stain.
        …mural paper on Center Academy art room wall competes with his story….

Girls have no story. I hum.

What is the real story?

your center cleared for
the solution seized to be wrung
or leaves plucked one by one
or marionette members strung
or wood-thrummed shelter from

the real meal of light sound sea
waves broken shored rhythms
scored to see bird caged in inn
or painting walled in home
or paned edifices moving vehicles

across state lines across countries
walled in continents to contain
first seed split so I am that I am
across first wooden bridge id centers
before sign warns return slowly after

animal origin repairs in wooden arc
to sustain the flood to seed
generations trained to believe
in all els elevated above down south
slaved to be

have
no
thing

I have

attached the tent's guts, Nancy directing.
Nancy's capable, Dick says,
drinking Bell's 12 on the rocks in his paper cup.

It collapses.

I stand on a solid rock in the mountain stream.
They reach for me to cross to their unstable rocks.
I reach for them to come to mine.

Deeper, I say to Alfie,
wanting him to say deeper words.
He dives deep into the stream. *I call*

the cinema of my sensibility…

My study is done,
or rather my point of departure is established,
then I let my pen run…

Nancy says this Maine road is like Easton road.
Like life always returning to the same familiar path.

Like life, Bud says, as a road we walk on splits.
We could go either way.

…where
it wills…

Fragments. Trying to find crumbs a child dropped
to return before home is the lie of this sun-filled ostensible.

My perfect family, homes, riches.

Alfie and I punch each other or Spaldings,
produce plays, share friends.

I teach Bud to drive, Nancy to walk.
I die when Dick leaves for boarding school.

This costume of words. This room. This set
table. This implied feast. I'm not whole.

A cocoon is hidden under the bridge.
The left side, below the troll.

   before clock brush pen racket
   arms hands fingers stroke
   body legs kick back

   before memory designs sign
   warning DO NOT MAKE
   FAST TO THIS BRIDGE

…Rothko gasped, yes, Dick was best. The real original.
The other kids painted the mural paper. Dick painted the wall.

Alfie painted hairless Rothko's assistant's pink head
red.

before circle returning five pink nudes to five naked
red androgynes

before Aspen day two reunion noon pink
doodles shuttle across Elizabeth Murray's red yell,

hide behind the boys,
I take a small intermission from Dick's oval table.

In Dick's black marble guest bathroom three gold
poles dangle three TV's with running movies plotting

comedy, drama…mystery...

of remembering
before

all members of all characters inside and out even the ones
who escaped but want to get back in even the ones locked in
who want out even the ones who went out even beyond
orange wafting from the lawn and its pond and garden
even further beyond the river running through

the dark forest arch opening even the ones deepest in
the basement by the vault looking out at the drywell
enclosed by the stone wall etched with the date this
cathedral was built for the whole congregation
taking communion or giving confessions of sin guilt

for rape incest war murder and conjugation of the original
nameless infinite nothing to be
inside the cardboard covers of childhood
an empty store somebody enters to sweep the floor
to build more shelves for more and more objects

needing 3D Technicolor to be
felt before the book is closed
forgotten real
estate finally
returning the adult

to ascend the stairs to lift the white sheets
off the furniture to descend to get out in
downtown fog lifting for the desperate one
we can see
from out here

is inside but so close to the pane
and on the phone
trying to call out
but the wire's too short
and it's been too long

Alfie knows how to get through childhood,
biking us to Coney Island,
taking me by subway to my city ballet,

then abandoning me,
who could never find my way,
on Broadway.

I remember your broken arm, I tell Bud.
You, eight, fell off the shed.
I fed you brisket, your favorite, mom and dad were out.

I was 10, he says.
Mom was in bed, a migraine day.
I sneaked a Coke.

...*if I am disturbed during the process I can no longer find the thread of it again.*

      so what is it to be re-
      turning to being re-

covered in my Manhattan Beach brick home to be re-
moved by somebody else familiar to Brighton Beach
to play myself out in somebody else's music

                Bach, no Handel's water music, no,
                country western, we all scream...

conducted in-out body-shaped instruments or sport implements
of the solution pooled right-angled to swim

                ...but Dick blares the *Trout Symphony*
                on his pool speakers, so Nancy, Alfie,
                Bud and I synchronize a ballet.

secret vaulted, darkness screened
moving images synthetic light projects to be inside

moving Coney Island vehicles to re-
call real feeling full circle

out in the open Cyclone cars to re-
member the fall

                        Fall! Dick claims he called on a
                        mountaintop to save me,
                        seven, skiing out of control
                        in Skiing, my first story. 1982.

We returned circling
strapped in Wonder

Wheel or Carousel
poled

up-down horses reaching for gold
rings

the real surf
left behind us

sitting eating Famous Nathan's hot dogs, fries watching across
Surf Avenue

Stillwell Terminal trains coming right to left
like Hebrew letters tell

in the beginning
heaven and earth split in

the Center
Academy third grade Hebrew class to begin

returning on parallel tracks
left to right

like the New
Testament word.

Once, Bud phoned from our Brooklyn home
being demolished. Mad, sad, taking bricks.

Once again, siblings, children, grandchildren
return to our abandoned Westport home.

Cold April day. White picket fence down.
Heat off. Floors un-rugged. Toilets clogged.

On our pine living room table below the paned
vista......   Dad is here, just outside this pane,

    tan, hairy chest, calves bulbous below blue
    Bermudas, prostrate on his patio chair,

    unaware of his dissolving mansion, engrossed
    in the one story he always returned to......

of terraced flagstone, green hills;...
    Decline and Fall
    of the Roman Empire......

we set out a final meal,
    ......Mom, upstairs, plucks a Pucci from
    the many we'll give our daughters,
    to wear her flare...

Passover leftovers
    ... from her closet......
    ......in their sleeping porch where

    wasps vibrating the screens......
We all vote no.
    ......have mysteriously disappeared......

But it's time to sell.
    ...But they emerge, like we will, too,
    in generations......

The sound

vibrating the screens...

Write it, Baba!
Simon's 11-year-old palm
softness in mine, 7/7/07.

Keep it going in your head
even when you're doing other things.
Stars ceiling our footsteps

on this wooden footbridge
across the Maine lake outlet.
But I don't want a life inside, I say.

Write it, he says.

Sign, Dick says, signs.

I had to find signs...

9/97 day two sibling reunion, 12:55 pm, contract, pens for five to sign to sell Westport, home. Dick's pool outside him inside his Aspen dining room... pool inside Matisse 1952 dining room inside 2014-5 MoMA...soprano in 1945 Shabbat dining room... birds caged...in inning 1 inn.

then everybody else signs,

...a collection of signs...

five closest relatives...around oval table...five...a round oval Dance... arms...hands...members...0...O...pens...identities...to seize seas... screen sss...scissor bodies...*feels like flight*...he says...

stands to leave each other to take flight

...signs...to discover myself...

sign, he says, write it, he says, live inside,
deeper, further back, root, match opposites,
stroke ball point pen characters

on different planes

...all this time I have searched...

to shoot kill sell steal base house hole goal
seed garden brick mansion block neighborhood out
in vehicle driven from home east west north south

across the United States to return home

...I discovered myself...

to be the original before fire before theft ancestors left
to return to rebuilt bigger one not to be
endless nothing to return to

…I remained the same…
                many rooms in many stories
*

The Sound

Now tilt the memory.
Stand further back.
The sound.

The same word repeats with new meaning.
Or extracts a latent one
as memory rises from the sea.

The sound the bell struck,
stuck in its somnolent ringing,
organizes the wound.

The sound. Since that time nothing has changed.
It has always been segmentation.
The visible is invisible embedded ringing.

Or something like this means
something like that
sea being recreated from silence.

Barbara Flug Colin's poems, essays and interviews appear in art, literary, teaching magazines and anthologies. She received 2012 Bechtel Prize, Notable Essay in The Best American Essays 2013, finalist in 2014 Diagram/New Michigan Essay Contest. Finishing Line Press published her first chapbook, *SWIMMING*.

www.ingramcontent.com/pod-product-compliance
Lightning Source LLC
Chambersburg PA
CBHW020831190426
43197CB00037B/1597